WookBooks
SWEET TREATS
RECIPE & COLORING BOOK

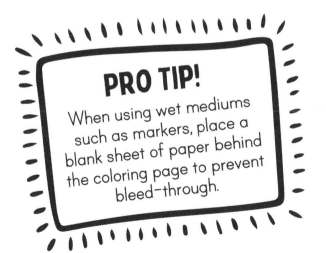

PRO TIP!

When using wet mediums such as markers, place a blank sheet of paper behind the coloring page to prevent bleed-through.

THANK YOU FOR YOUR PURCHASE!

This book belongs to:

_____

_____

_____

OOEY GOOEY
CHOCOLATE CHIP COOKIES

yummies: 1 c. butter, 1/4 c. white sugar, 1 1/4 c. dark brown sugar, 2 eggs, 2 tsp. vanilla extract, 2 1/2 c. flour, 1 tsp. baking soda, 1/2 tsp. salt, 2 c. semi-sweet chocolate chips. preheat oven to 350 degrees. in large bowl, cream together softened butter and sugars until fluffy. stir in vanilla, salt, and baking soda. gently stir in flour as to not overmix. fold in chocolate chips. drop spoonfuls of the dough onto an ungreased baking sheet. bake 8-10 mins. enjoy!

GOLDEN
FRENCH TOAST

yummies: 1/4 c. flour, 1 c. milk, 3 eggs, 1 tbsp. sugar, 1 tsp. vanilla, 1/2 tsp. ground cinnamon, 1 pinch salt, 12 thick slices of bread. measure flour into a mixing bowl. slowly whisk in milk. whisk in eggs, sugar, vanilla, cinnamon, and salt until smooth. heat a lightly oiled griddle over medium heat. meanwhile, soak bread slices in milk mixture until saturated. working in batches, cook bread on the griddle until golden brown on each side. serve with butter, powdered sugar, and fresh fruit. enjoy!

WHITE CHOCOLATE
BLUEBERRY OATMEAL COOKIES

yummies: 1 1/4 c. flour, 3/4 c. old fashioned oats, 1/2 tsp. cinnamon, 1/2 tsp. baking powder, 1/8 tsp. baking soda, pinch salt, 1/2 c. butter, 3/4 c. brown sugar, 1 tsp. vanilla, 1 egg, 1/2 c. white chocolate chips, 1/2 c. blueberries. preheat oven to 350 degrees. in a medium bowl combine flour, oats, cinnamon, baking powder, baking soda, salt. beat butter and sugar until fluffy. beat in vanilla and egg. gently mix in flour mixture until just incorporated taking care not to over mix. fold in chocolate chips and blueberries. drop tablespoons of batter onto a parchment paper lined baking sheet. flatten just a bit. bake 7-8 mins. cool and enjoy!

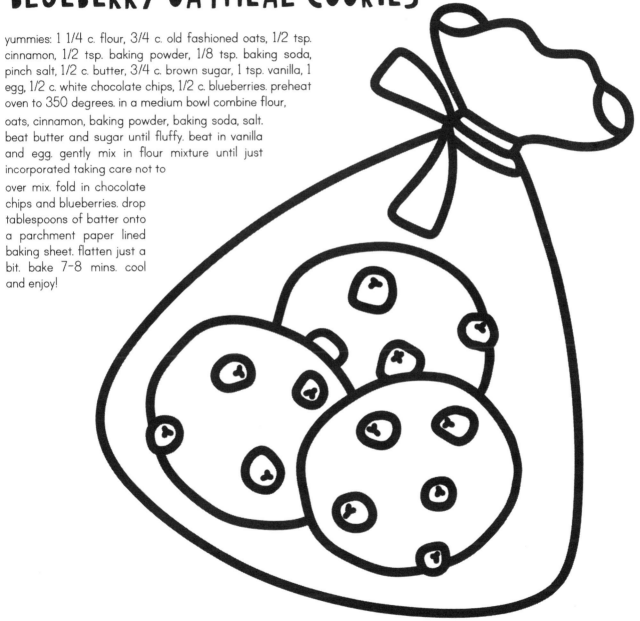

VELVETY HOT COCOA

yummies: 4 c. whole milk, 1/4 c. unsweetened cocoa powder, 1/4 c. sugar, 1/2 c. semisweet chocolate chips, 1/4 tsp. vanilla. warm milk, cocoa powder, and sugar in a small saucepan over medium-low heat, whisking frequently. do not boil. add chocolate chips and whisk constantly until fully incorporated. whisk in vanilla. serve in a cozy mug topped with fluffy marshmallows. enjoy!

PECAN
TASSIES

yummies: crust dough: 3 oz. softened cream cheese, 1 c. flour, 1/2 c. softened butter. filling: 2 eggs, 1 1/2 cup brown sugar, 1 tsp. vanilla, 1/2 c. chopped pecans, 2 tblsp. melted butter. preheat oven to 350 degrees. hand mix dough ingredients. roll into 1 inch balls. press into mini muffin pan creating little wells for the filling. mix filling ingredients, adding the melted butter last. spoon mixture into the dough wells. do not overfill. bake for 22 minutes. use a fork to remove pecan tassies from pan. enjoy!

CHEWY
HONEY COOKIES

yummies: 1 c. softened unsalted butter, 1 c. sugar, 1/4 c. brown sugar, 1/3 c. honey, 1 tsp. vanilla, 1 egg, 3 c. flour, 2 tsp. cornstarch, 1 tsp. baking powder, 1/2 tsp. baking soda, 3/4 tsp. salt, 1/2 c. granulated sugar for rolling. in a large bowl, combine butter, sugars, honey, and vanilla. beat until well combined. add egg and stir well. in a separate bowl, whisk together flour, cornstarch, baking powder, baking soda, and salt.

gently add flour mixture to butter mixture and mix until completely combined. cover and refrigerate for at least 1 hour. preheat oven to 375 degrees. scoop dough into 1 1/2 tablespoon portions. roll into smooth balls, then roll through granulated sugar. place 2 inches apart on a parchment paper lined cookie sheet. bake cookies about 10 minutes, until edges begin to turn a light brown. allow cookies to cool 10 minutes before removing from baking sheet. enjoy!

SPRINKLED CAKE POPS

yummies: 24 cake pop sticks, 1 prepared 9x13 cake, 10 oz. dark chocolate melting wafers, 10 oz. white chocolate melting wafers, 1 stick salted butter, 2 1/2 c. powdered sugar, 1 tsp. vanilla, 1 tbsp. heavy cream, sprinkles. first make the buttercream frosting. in a medium bowl, whip the butter. add the powdered sugar and mix until combined. add the vanilla and cream. next, assemble the cake pops. in a large bowl, using your hands crumble the prepared cake into fine crumbs. add 2 spoonfuls of buttercream frosting to the cake. gradually add more frosting until the cake holds together when squeezed. roll the dough into cake pop balls. freeze balls for 10 minutes. meanwhile, melt the dark and white chocolate in separate tall narrow jars. dip each cake pop stick onto the melted chocolate then into the center of the cake pop. return to fridge to set. once set, dip the cake pops into the melted chocolate. add sprinkles. push cake pop stick into a styrofoam block for about an hour to set. enjoy!

1

BANANA
PUDDING TRIFLE

yummies: 8 oz. cream cheese at room temperature, 14 oz. can of sweetened condensed milk, 1 c. milk, 3.4 oz. package of instant vanilla pudding, 16 oz. cool whip, 11 oz. box of vanilla wafers, 3 bananas sliced into rounds. beat the cream cheese until smooth. add condensed milk, milk, and pudding mix. beat on high for 2 minutes. fold in half the cool whip. begin assembling the trifle by layering 1/3 pudding mix, vanilla wafers, bananas, half of remaining pudding, vanilla wafers, bananas, remaining pudding, wafers, remaining cool whip. refrigerate at least 2 hours before enjoying.

FIZZY
ITALIAN SODA

yummies: 4 tblsp. flavored syrup of your choice, 1 c. ice, 16 oz. club soda, 1 tblsp. heavy cream, maraschino cherries or other fruit toppings of your choice such as pineapple, lemon, lime, or mango. using a tall clear glass, add in any combination of flavored syrups, about 3 tblsp. in total. add in ice. fill with club soda. top with a drizzle of cream. top with maraschino cherry or other toppings of your choice.

LEMON
POUND CAKE

yummies: cake: 1 1/2 c. flour, 1 1/2 tsp. baking powder, 1/2 tsp. salt, 1 c. unsalted butter, 1 c. sugar, 3 eggs, 1/4 c. sour cream, 1 tsp. lemon zest, 3 tblsp. fresh squeezed lemon juice, 1 tsp. vanilla. icing: 1 c. powdered sugar, 1 1/2 tblsp. lemon juice, 1 tblsp. heavy cream. lower oven rack to lower-third position and preheat oven to 350 degrees. grease loaf pan with nonstick spray. make the cake: whisk the flour, baking powder, and salt in a large bowl. set aside. beat butter and sugar until fluffy. add in one egg at a time. add sour cream, lemon juice, lemon zest, and vanilla. beat until combined. gently stir in dry ingredients until just combined. do not overmix. pour batter into prepared loaf pan and cook 60 mins. tent the cake with aluminum foil halfway through to avoid overbrowning. cool on a wire rack for an hour before removing from pan. meanwhile, make the icing. whisk all ingredients together. pour over cooled cake. enjoy!

CINNAMON
DUSTED CHURROS

yummies: 1 c. water, 1/4 c. unsalted butter diced into small cubes, 1 tbsp. sugar, 1/4 tsp. salt, 1 c. flour, 1 egg, 1/2 tsp. vanilla, vegetable oil for frying. for the coating, whisk together 1/2 c. sugar, 3/4 tsp. ground cinnamon, and set aside. heat 2 inches of vegetable oil in a large pot to 360 degrees. separately, add water, butter, sugar and salt to a large saucepan, bring to a boil. add flour and reduce heat to medium low while stirring constantly with a rubber spatula until smooth. transfer mixture to a large bowl and cool 5 minutes. add vanilla and egg to the flour mixture and blend with an electric blender until smooth. transfer to a piping bag with a rounded star tip no larger than 1/2 inch. carefully pipe mixture into 6-inch lengths, cutting with clean scissors, directly into hot oil. let fry until golden brown, about 2 minutes per side. transfer to a paper towel lined plate to dry briefly, then transfer to cinnamon sugar mixture and roll to coat. serve plain or with chocolate dipping sauce. enjoy!

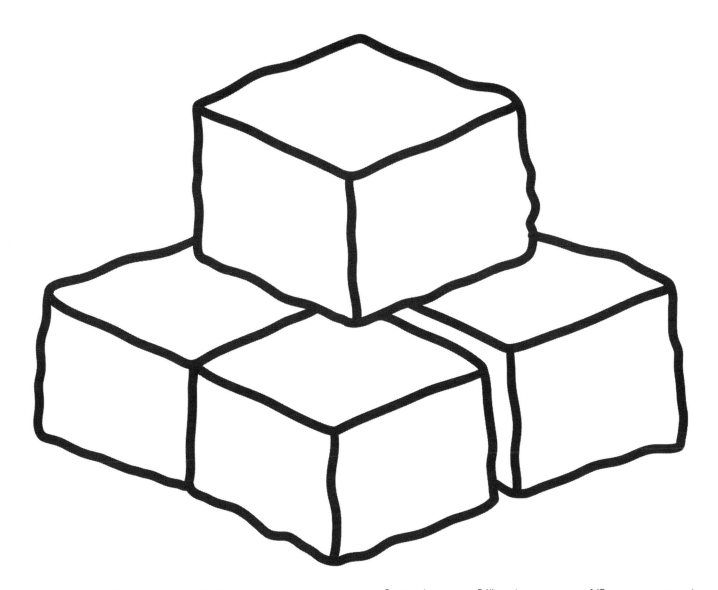

EXTRA FUDGY
MIDNIGHT BANANA BROWNIES

yummies: 3 ripe bananas, 3/4 c. brown sugar, 1/2 c. unsweetened apple sauce, 1 tsp. vanilla, 1 egg, 1 c. flour, 1/2 c. extra dark unsweetened cocoa powder, 1 tsp. baking soda, 1/2 tsp salt, 1 c. semi-sweet chocolate chips. preheat oven to 350 degrees. with an electric or stand mixer, mix together bananas and brown sugar. mix in applesauce, vanilla, and egg. in a separate bowl, whisk together the flour, cocoa, baking soda, and salt. fold dry mixture into wet mixture. fold in chocolate chips. pour batter into a greased 8x8 baking pan. press a few extra chocolate chips on the top. bake for about 45 minutes. cool and enjoy!

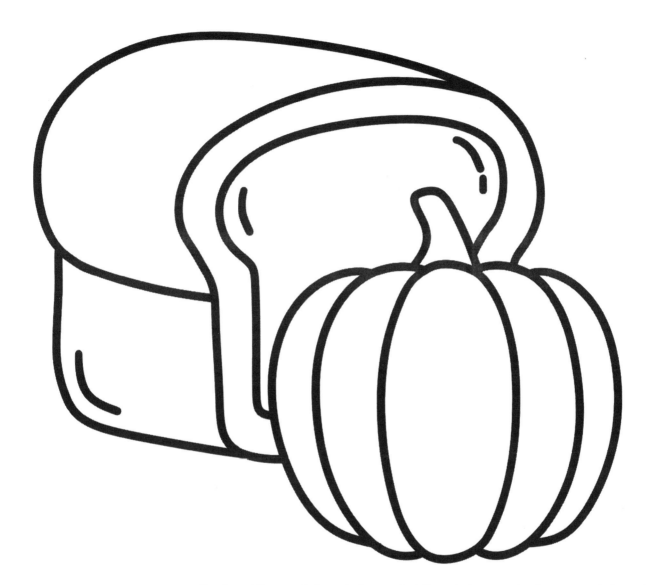

SPICED
PUMPKIN BREAD

yummies: 2 c. flour, 1/2 tsp. salt, 1 tsp. baking soda, 1/2 tsp. baking powder, 1 tsp. ground cloves, 1 tsp. ground cinnamon, 1 tsp. nutmeg, 1 1/2 sticks unsalted butter, 2 c. sugar, 2 eggs, 1 fifteen oz. can of 100% pumpkin puree. preheat oven to 325 degrees with rack positioned in the center of the oven. use butter to grease two loaf pans. dust loaf pans with flour. in a medium bowl, whisk together all dry ingredients. set aside. in a large bowl, beat the butter and sugar until just blended. add in one egg at a time. continue beating until light and fluffy. beat in pumpkin. on low speed, add the dry ingredient mixture, taking care to not over mix. divide batter between the two prepared loaf pans. bake 65 minutes, turn finished loaves onto a wire rack to cool. enjoy!

KRISPIE
RICE TREATS

yummies: 1/4 c. butter, 4 c. miniature marshmallows, 5 c. crispy rice cereal. melt butter in a large saucepan over low heat. add marshmallows and stir until melted and well combined. cook 2 minutes longer, stirring constantly. remove from heat. stir in crispy rice cereal until well coated. press mixture evenly and firmly into a buttered 9x13-inch pan using a buttered spatula or waxed paper. cut into squares when cool. enjoy!

1

TANGY
LEMON CUSTARD

yummies: 1/4 c. fresh lemon juice, 1 tblsp. lemon zest, 2/3 c. sugar, 3 1/2 tblsp. cornstarch, 4 egg yolks, 2 1/3 c. milk, 3/4 c. light cream, 2 tblsp. butter, 1 tsp. vanilla. place sugar, cornstarch, and lemon zest in a medium saucepan, whisk to combine. whisk in egg yolks, milk, and cream. heat over medium-low heat, whisking until thickened and starting to boil, about 15 minutes. once boiling, let bubble for 1 minute while whisking. remove from heat and add in butter, lemon juice, and vanilla. pour into a jar. cover with plastic wrap, resting the wrap on the surface of the custard. refrigerate at least 2 hours. Serve cold and enjoy!

GRANDMA'S
FLAKIEST CRUST APPLE PIE

yummies: crust: 2 c. flour, 1 tsp. salt, 2/3 c. shortening, 4 tblsp. cold butter, 5 tblsp. ice water. filling: 5 macintosh apples cored and sliced into thin 1/4-inch slices, 1/2 tsp. ground cinnamon, 1/4 tsp. ground nutmeg, 1/2 c. sugar, 1/2 c. flour. first make the crust. keeping as cold as possible, cut butter and shortening into flour and salt using a pastry cutter until pea sized. add water and mix by hand forming two round dough balls. keep dough as cold as possible at all times. saranwrap and refrigerate the 2 dough balls for 60 minutes. make filling. mix thinly sliced apples with flour, cinnamon, nutmeg, and sugar. butter a glass pie pan. rollout each dough ball on floured surface until thin, about 1/4 inch. gently lay one dough sheet into pie pan. poke holes in the bottom to release steam. fill with apple mixture. top with dabs of butter. gently lay second dough sheet over filled pie pan. tuck edges under and use fingers to crimp the edges. cut a small slit on top. cover crust edges with tinfoil. bake for 40 minutes, removing the tinfoil from the crust for the last 15 minutes. cool, slice, and enjoy!

CHEWY MACARONS

yummies: cookies: 3 egg whites, 1 1/2 c. almond flour, 1/2 c. granulated sugar, 1 c. powdered sugar, 1 tsp. vanilla, 1/4 tsp. cream of tartar. buttercream icing: 1 c. unsalted butter, 5 egg yolks, 1/2 c. granulated sugar, 1 tsp. vanilla, 3 tblsp. water, and a pinch of salt. first make the cookies. sift the powdered sugar and almond flour into a bowl. in a separate bowl, add egg whites. using an electric mixer, whisk eggs until they begin to foam. slowly add cream of tartar and then slowly add granulated sugar. add vanilla and food coloring if desired. continue to beat until stiff peaks form. begin folding in dry ingredients in batches. thoroughly combine. spoon into a piping bag with a medium round tip. pipe 1-inch dollops onto a baking sheet lined with parchment paper. tap on counter several times to release air bubbles. allow to sit for 40 minutes before placing in oven. bake at 300 degrees for 12-15 minutes. allow to cool completely before removing from baking sheet. next, make the buttercream icing. combine sugar and water in medium saucepan over low heat, stirring until sugar dissolves. increase heat to medium-high and bring to a boil. beat egg yolks until thick and foamy. slowly drizzle boiling sugar water into bowl with yolks. continue mixing until mixture has cooled to room temperature. add in butter one cube at a time. add vanilla and salt. continue mixing until smooth and creamy. pipe filling into the back of half the cookie shells, forming a sandwich. store in the refrigerator. enjoy!

EASY
WAFFLES

yummies: 1 c. flour, 2 tsp. baking powder, 1 tsp. sugar, 1/4 tsp. salt, 1 c. milk, 1/4 c. melted butter, 1 egg separated. heat the waffle iron. mix flour, baking powder, sugar, and salt in a medium bowl. stir in milk, butter, and egg yolk until blended. beat egg white in a small bowl on high speed until stiff peaks form. fold into batter. pour about 3/4 c. of the batter onto the center of a hot waffle iron. bake until steaming stops. remove from iron. top with syrup or whipped cream and fruit. enjoy!

CLASSIC
PUMPKIN PIE

yummies: 1 fifteen oz. can pumpkin puree, 1 fourteen oz. can sweetened condensed milk, 2 eggs, 1 tsp. ground cinnamon, 1/2 tsp. ground ginger, 1/2 tsp. ground nutmeg, 1/2 tsp. salt, 1 nine-inch unbaked pie crust. preheat the oven to 425 degrees. whisk pumpkin puree, condensed milk, eggs, cinnamon, nutmeg, ginger, and salt together in a medium bowl until smooth. pour into crust. bake for 15 mins. reduce oven temperature to 350 degrees. continue baking for 35-40 mins. once fully cool, top with fresh whipped cream and serve.

WARM
CINNAMON ROLLS

yummies: dough: 2 3/4 c. flour, 1/4 c. granulated sugar, 1/2 tsp. salt, 3/4 c. milk, 3 tblsp. unsalted butter, 2 1/3 tsp. instant yeast, 1 egg. filling: 3 tblsp. soft unsalted butter, 1/3 c. brown sugar, 1 tblsp. ground cinnamon. cream cheese frosting: 4 oz. softened cream cheese, 2 tblsp. unsalted butter, 2/3 c. powdered sugar, 1 tsp. vanilla. make the dough. whisk the flour, sugar, and salt together in a bowl. set aside. combine milk and butter together in a heatproof bowl and microwave until butter has melted and milk is warm, not hot. whisk in the yeast until it has dissolved. pour mixture into dry ingredients, add in the egg and stir until a soft dough forms. transfer dough to a lightly floured surface and knead for about 5 minutes. the dough should be smooth. place dough in a lightly greased bowl and cover loosely. let the dough rest for 10 minutes. after 10 minutes, roll the dough out into a 14x8 rectangle.

spread softened butter on top dough. mix together the cinnamon and brown sugar and sprinkle all over the dough. roll up the dough to make a 14-inch log. cut into 10-12 even rolls and arrange in a lightly greased 9-inch round pie pan. cover the pan with a clean kitchen towel and allow rolls to rise, about 90 minutes. preheat oven to 375 degrees. bake rolls for 25 minutes, or until browned. make the icing. beat cream cheese on high until smooth. add butter and beat until combined. beat in powdered sugar and vanilla. spread icing over the warm rolls and serve immediately. enjoy!

WARM SPICED
GINGERBREAD COOKIES

yummies: 1/2 c. sugar, 1/2 c. shortening, 1/2 c. dark molasses, 1/4 c. water, 3/4 tsp. salt, 3/4 tsp. ground ginger, 1/2 tsp baking soda, 1/4 tsp. ground allspice, 2 1/2 c. flour. beat sugar, shortening, molasses, and water in a large bowl on low speed until blended. stir in remaining ingredients. cover and refrigerate until chilled. heat oven to 375 degrees. on a flour dusted surface, roll out dough with a rolling pin until 1/4 in. thick. cut with gingerbread man shaped cutters. bake for 8-10 minutes on an ungreased cookie sheet. cool and decorate to bring your gingerbread man to life. enjoy!

EASY DONUTS

yummies: 3 1/2 c. flour, 3/4 c. sugar, 1/2 tsp. baking soda, 2 tsp. baking powder, 1 tsp. salt, 1 tsp. ground cinnamon, 1/2 tsp. ground nutmeg, 3/4 c. buttermilk, 1/4 c. melted butter, 1 tsp. vanilla, 2 eggs, vegetable oil for frying. fill a pan with about 1 inch of vegetable oil then line a baking tray with a wire rack and paper towel for the donuts to cool. in a medium bowl, combine the flour, sugar, baking powder, baking soda, salt, and spices. set aside. in another bowl, combine buttermilk, melted butter, vanilla, and eggs. gradually whisk the dry ingredients into the wet until a sticky dough has formed. transfer dough to a lightly floured work surface and bring the dough together with your hands. press dough into a 12-inch rectangle about 1.2 inch thick. before cutting dough, heat oil over medium-low heat for about 5 minutes. while oil is heating, cut out your donuts using a 3-inch round cookie cutter. carefully drop the donuts into the oil and fry for about 3 minutes per side. remove from pan and allow donuts to cool on prepared cooling rack. toss in cinnamon sugar or coat with a glaze. enjoy!

CONFETTI
BIRTHDAY CAKE

yummies: 3 3/4 c. cake flour, 1 tsp. baking powder, 1 tsp. baking soda, 1 tsp. salt, 1 1/4 c. unsalted softened butter, 2 c. sugar, 1/3 c. vegetable oil, 4 eggs, 2 egg whites, 3 tsp. vanilla, 1 1/2 c. room temperature buttermilk, 3/4 c. rainbow sprinkles. preheat oven to 350 degrees. grease three 8-inch cake pans and line with parchment paper rounds. whisk the cake flour, baking powder, baking soda, and salt together in a large bowl. set aside. beat the butter and sugar together on high speed for 5 minutes. add the oil and beat for 1 minute. add the eggs, egg whites, and vanilla extract.

add dry ingredients and buttermilk in three additions, mixing after each addition until just incorporated. gently fold in the sprinkles. pour the batter evenly into the cake pans. bake for 25 minutes or until baked through. to test doneness, insert a toothpick into the center of the cake. if it comes out clean then it's done. allow cakes to cool in pan for 20 minutes. carefully remove cake from pans and allow to fully cool on cooling rack. assemble and frost with your choice of icing. don't forget the sprinkles!

HOMEMADE
FRUIT POPSICLES

yummies: 3/4 c. yogurt or juice, 2 1/2 c. fruit, 6 tblsp. honey, 1/4 tsp. vanilla, 1/2 tsp. lemon juice. add all ingredients to a blender. blend until mixture is smooth, about 1 minute. evenly distribute the mixture into the wells of a popsicle mold. secure the lids and sticks on top of the mold and freeze overnight. remove molds, run each one under hot water for 30 seconds. enjoy immediately or freeze in an airtight bag.

ULTIMATE BANANA SPLIT

yummies: 1 banana peeled and split lengthwise, 1 scoop vanilla ice cream, 1 scoop chocolate ice cream, 1 scoop strawberry ice cream, 2 tblsp. fresh diced pineapple, 2 tblsp. hot fudge, 2 tblsp. fresh diced strawberries, whipped cream, 3 maraschino cherries, 2 tblsp. chopped peanuts. place banana slices sideways against the sides of a long shallow dish. place the ice cream scoops in a row between the banana slices. spoon the pineapple over the vanilla ice cream. drizzle the fudge over the chocolate ice cream. spoon the strawberries over the strawberry ice cream. top each scoop of ice cream with a dollop of whipped cream and a cherry. garnish with a sprinkle of chopped nuts. serve and enjoy!

TASTY
DIRT AND WORMS

yummies: 12 chocolate cream-filled cookies, 3.9 oz package instant chocolate pudding mix, 2 c. milk, 3 oz. package gummy worms candy. place cookies in a plastic bag and crush with a rolling pin into crumbs. whisk together pudding mix with milk in a bowl, stirring for 2 minutes. sprinkle about 1/3 of the crushed cookie crumbs into the bottom of a serving bowl and spoon chocolate pudding over crumbs. smooth out the top of the pudding, then top with the rest of the crumbled cookies to resemble dirt. arrange gummy worms halfway into the dirt. refrigerate until serving.

CHEWY
PEANUT BUTTER COOKIES

yummies: 1 1/2 c. flour, 1/2 c. unsalted butter, 1 c. peanut butter, 1/2 c. brown sugar, 1/2 c. sugar, 1 tsp. vanilla, 1 egg, 3/4 tsp. baking powder. preheat oven to 350 degrees. sift flour and baking power together then whisk to combine. cream butter and sugars with a mixer. add peanut butter and mix until incorporated. mix in egg and vanilla then add flour. roll dough into one inch balls an place on baking sheet lined with parchment paper. flatten cookies with a fork in a crisscross pattern. bake for 10 minutes. allow cookies to cool completely before removing from baking sheet. enjoy!

BUBBLE BOBA TEA

yummies: boba: 10 c. filtered water, 1 2/3 c. black tapioca pearls, 4 tblsp. brown sugar. milk tea: 4 c. boiling water, 8 black tea bags, 4 c. ice, 1/2 c. simple syrup, and 1/2 c. half and half. for the boba, add the water to a 5-quart pot and bring to a boil. once the water is boiling, add the tapioca pearls and boil for 20 minutes. after boiling, reserve 1 1/2 c. of the cooking fluid, and then rinse and drain the boba. put the boba back in the pot. stir in the reserved cooking liquid and the brown sugar. cover the pot and let steep for 20 minutes. drain the boba except for 2 tblsp. of the liquid to prevent boba from sticking together. while the boba is cooking, make the tea. add the water to the saucepan and bring to a boil. remove from heat and add the tea bags. let steep until it cools to room temperature. remove tea bags. divide the ice between 4 glasses and add 1/4 of the cooled tea, simple syrup, and half and half to each glass. top each with 1/2 c. boba. enjoy immediately!

FESTIVE YULE LOG

yummies: 6 eggs, 1 box chocolate cake mix, 1/3 c. water, 1/4 c. vegetable oil, 1 tblsp. powdered sugar, 12 oz. fluffy marshmallow frosting, 12 oz. whipped chocolate frosting, fresh cranberries and rosemary for garnish. in a large bowl, beat eggs for 5 minutes until pale in color. add cake mix, water, and oil and beat on low for 2 minutes. line a baking pan then coat the liner with baking spray. make sure to grease sides of the pan. pour batter onto prepared 12x18 baking pan. bake at 350 for 15 minutes. remove from oven and let cool for 10 minutes. while the cake is still warm, grab a linen dish towel. sprinkle both sides of the towel with powdered sugar, then lay it on top the cake. gently flip the cake upside down so that it drops into the dish towel. lay on a clean surface and peel off the liner. tightly but gently roll the cake, keeping the towel in place to separate the layers. place the roll on a cooking rack and let cool at least 15 minutes. when cooled, gently unroll the cake and spread with marshmallow frosting. roll the cake to form a log. frost outside and ends with chocolate frosting. using a fork, create a bark-like pattern in the frosting and garnish with cranberries and rosemary. enjoy!

SWEET CANNOLIS

yummies: 8 cannoli shells, 2 c. ricotta cheese, 1 c. powdered sugar, 3/4 c. mini chocolate chips, 1 1/2 tsp. vanilla, 2 tsp. orange zest. place the ricotta cheese into a fine mesh strainer and place it in the fridge to drain for at least 12 hours. in a large bowl, combine the drained ricotta, powdered sugar, 1/4 c. of the mini chocolate chips, vanilla, and orange zest. using a spatula, scrape mixture into pastry bag fitted with 1/2-inch open tip. when ready to serve, pipe the filling into one end of cannoli shell, filling halfway, then pipe into the other end. place remaining chocolate chips on a plate and dip each end of the cannoli into the chips. dust lightly with powdered sugar. enjoy immediately!

STRAWBERRY SHORT CAKE

yummies: 1 qt. fresh sliced strawberries, 1/4 c. powdered sugar, 1 prepared boxed angel food cake, whipped cream. place strawberries in a bowl. add sugar and stir to coat. allow to marinate 15 minutes. cut prepared angel food cake into generous slices. top cake with sugared strawberries and whipped cream. enjoy!

CHOCOLATE
COVERED STRAWBERRIES

yummies: 10 oz. chocolate baking chips, 2 lbs. fresh strawberries. wash strawberries thoroughly. dry strawberries completely. line a pan with parchment paper. microwave the chocolate for 30 second intervals, removing and stirring at each 30 second interval, until chocolate has melted. holding the strawberry stem, dip into melted chocolate. at this point, you may dip strawberries into toppings such as coconut, nuts, or sprinkles. place the strawberries on the parchment paper. for white chocolate drizzled strawberries, dip a fork in the melted white chocolate and drizzle over strawberries. chill until the chocolate sets, about 15 minutes. enjoy!

SUGARED
BLUEBERRY MUFFINS

yummies: 1 1/2 c. flour, 3/4 c. sugar, 2 tsp. baking powder, 1/4 tsp. salt, 1/3 c. vegetable oil, 1 egg, 1/3 c. milk, 1 1/2 tsp. vanilla, 1 c. blueberries. preheat oven to 400 degrees. line muffin cups with paper liners. whisk the flour, sugar, baking powder, and salt in a large bowl. stir in oil, egg, milk and vanilla. do not overmix. gently fold in blueberries. divide batter between muffin cups. sprinkle a little extra sugar on the tops of each muffin. bake 15-20 minutes, or until tops are no longer wet and a toothpick inserted into the middle of a muffin comes out with crumbs. transfer to a cooling rack. enjoy with a dab of butter.

TRAITIONAL SPANISH FLAN

yummies: 1 c. sugar, 3 large eggs, 14 oz. can condensed milk, 12 oz. can evaporated milk, 1 tblsp. vanilla. preheat oven to 350 degrees. melt sugar in a medium saucepan over medium-low heat until liquified and golden. carefully pour hot syrup into a deep 9-inch round glass baking dish, turning the dish to evenly coat the bottom. set aside. beat eggs in a large bowl. add condensed milk, evaporated milk, and vanilla. beat until smooth. pour egg mixture on top of caramel in the baking dish. place in a deep roasting pan. carefully pour enough hot water to come 1-inch up the sides of the roasting pan. bake 1 hour. cool to room temperature, then cover with plastic wrap to prevent a skin from forming. refrigerate 3 hours. enjoy!

PINEAPPLE
UPSIDE DOWN CAKE

yummies: topping: 1/4 c. melted butter, 1/2 c. brown sugar, 10 pineapple slices, maraschino cherries. vanilla cake: 1/2 c. unsalted butter, 3/4 c. sugar, 2 eggs, 1 tsp. vanilla, 1 1/2 c. flour, 1 1/2 tsp. baking powder, 1/4 tsp. salt, 1/2 c. milk. preheat oven to 350 degrees. pour melted butter into 10-inch pie pan taking care to cover the entire bottom and grease sides of the pan. sprinkle brown sugar evenly over butter. arrange pineapple slices over bottom of pan and up the sides, slicing as necessary. place cherries in the center of the pineapple rings. prepare cake. beat butter and sugar until fluffy. add eggs one at a time. stir in vanilla. in a separate bowl, whisk together flour, baking powder, and salt. alternate adding flour and milk to the wet ingredients, starting and ending with flour. do not overmix. pour batter over prepared pie pan. bake for 30 minutes. at the 30-minute mark, loosely cover with foil and continue to bake for another 15 minutes. allow to cool for 15 minutes, then carefully invert cake onto serving platter. cool fully, cut, and enjoy!

RECIPE:

_____

_____

_____

_____

_____

_____

_____

_____

_____

_____

RECIPE:

RECIPE:

_____

_____

_____

_____

_____

_____

_____

_____

_____

_____

RECIPE:

_____

_____

_____

_____

_____

_____

_____

_____

_____

_____

RECIPE:

_____

_____

_____

_____

_____

_____

_____

_____

_____

_____

Made in the USA
Columbia, SC
29 October 2024

44707207R00048